DISCOVERING ACADIA

A GUIDE FOR YOUNG NATURALISTS

Written and Illustrated by

MARGARET SCHEID

ISBN 0-934745-04-8
LIBRARY OF CONGRESS CATALOG CARD NUMBER 86-71350

ACADIA PRESS
ACADIA PUBLISHING COMPANY
P.O. BOX 170
BAR HARBOR, MAINE 04609

SECOND PRINTING - JULY, 1988 - PRINTED IN THE U.S.A.

~ ~ ~ ~ ~ ~ ~ ~

ACKNOWLEDGEMENTS
I THANK THE FOLLOWING PEOPLE
FOR THEIR CONTRIBUTIONS TO THIS BOOK:
PETER CORCORAN AND SENTIEL ROMMEL, FOR
THEIR ENTHUSIASM AND ADVICE ON THE ORIGINAL DRAFT;
LOIS WINTER, WHOSE CAREFUL EDITING, PATIENCE, AND SUPPORT
HELPED MAKE THIS BOOK POSSIBLE; AND THE STAFF OF PHOTOTYPE
ENGRAVING COMPANY, FOR THEIR COMMITMENT TO EXCELLENCE AND
QUALITY REPRODUCTION. FINALLY, I THANK JEANNINE ROSS, HEIDI WELCH,
MY FAMILY, AND FRIENDS FOR THEIR HELP AND ENCOURAGEMENT.

thank you all!

meg

for my parents ♥

WHAT IS A NATURALIST?

AS A NATURALIST, YOU ENJOY KNOWING AND LEARNING ABOUT THE OUTDOORS!

YOU MIGHT FOLLOW AN ANIMAL'S TRACKS . . . A FIREFLY'S FLASH . . . OR WONDER WHAT SURPRISES LURK IN THE SALTY SEAWEEDS!

AS YOU LEARN MORE, YOU'LL UNDERSTAND IT'S IMPORTANT TO CARE FOR THE NATURAL WORLD.

SOON YOU'LL DISCOVER THAT WE TOO ARE PART OF NATURE. BY TAKING CARE OF NATURE, WE TAKE CARE OF OURSELVES!

1

MY NAME IS

I AM A YOUNG NATURALIST

AND FRIEND OF ACADIA

MY PROMISE

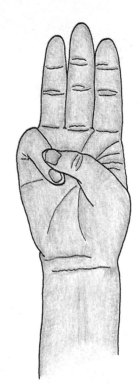

I, _____, PROMISE TO DO MY BEST TO BE A FRIEND OF NATURE IN ACADIA NATIONAL PARK AND WHEREVER ELSE I GO.

I PROMISE THAT I WILL NOT INTENTIONALLY POLLUTE, DESTROY, FRIGHTEN, OR HARM PLANTS OR ANIMALS, HOWEVER BIG OR SMALL. I REALIZE MY ACTIONS WILL BE AN EXAMPLE TO OTHER PEOPLE, OLDER & YOUNGER.

I PROMISE NOT TO DESTROY NATURE WHILE I ENJOY NATURE.

SIGNED _____

WITNESS _____

DATE _____

 CONTENTS

5

1

TREE TIPS

DON'T FORGET!

- USE PAGE 29 FOR TRACING,
  LABELING, AND REMEMBERING
  YOUR FAVORITE LEAVES.
- BE SURE TO BRING A PENCIL.

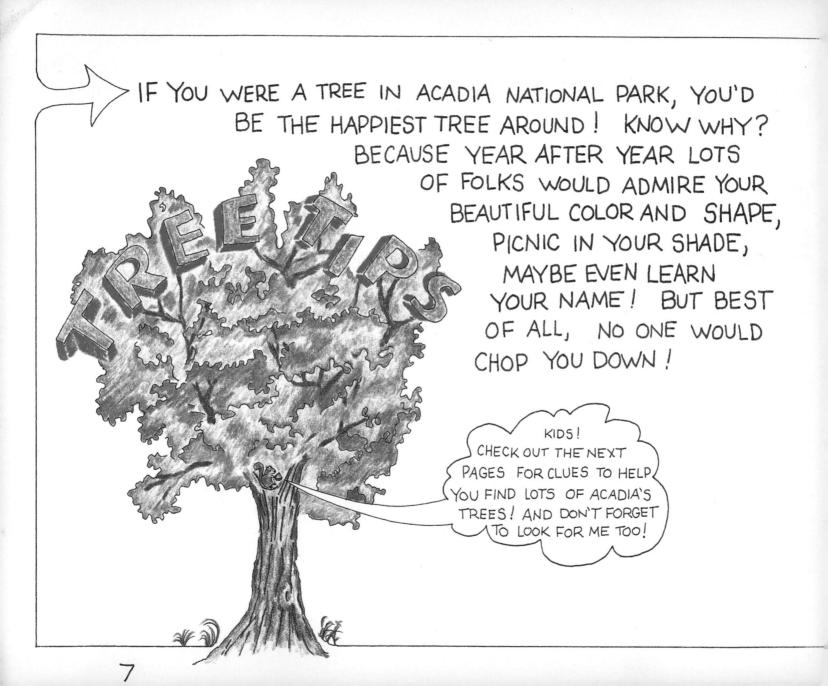

IF YOU WERE A TREE IN ACADIA NATIONAL PARK, YOU'D BE THE HAPPIEST TREE AROUND! KNOW WHY? BECAUSE YEAR AFTER YEAR LOTS OF FOLKS WOULD ADMIRE YOUR BEAUTIFUL COLOR AND SHAPE, PICNIC IN YOUR SHADE, MAYBE EVEN LEARN YOUR NAME! BUT BEST OF ALL, NO ONE WOULD CHOP YOU DOWN!

KIDS! CHECK OUT THE NEXT PAGES FOR CLUES TO HELP YOU FIND LOTS OF ACADIA'S TREES! AND DON'T FORGET TO LOOK FOR ME TOO!

THE TWO KINDS OF TREES THAT GROW IN ACADIA ARE EASY TO TELL APART.

 DECIDUOUS TREES
(DE-SID-YOU-US)

THESE TREES DROP THEIR
LEAVES IN THE FALL, LIKE
THE MAPLE TREES.

 CONIFEROUS TREES
(CONE-IF-ER-US)

THESE TREES GROW CONES,
LIKE THE PINE TREES.

HAVE YOU EVER HEARD OF A DECIDUOUS-CONIFER? IF NOT, DON'T LOOK ON PAGE 26; YOU MIGHT HAVE A TAMARACK ATTACK!!

TURN THE PAGE TO MEET THE DECIDUOUS TREES!

DECIDUOUS TREES

DROP THEIR LEAVES IN THE FALL.

HOW MANY KINDS OF DECIDUOUS TREES ARE IN ACADIA?
(ABOUT 40)
WAY TOO MANY
TO PUT IN THIS BOOK!

SO, LET'S LOOK FOR **SIX** OF THE MOST COMMON TREES:

YOU CAN ALSO CALL US BROAD-LEAVED TREES!

RUSSELL

OAK   MAPLE   ASPEN   BEECH   BIRCH   ASH

FALL COLORS

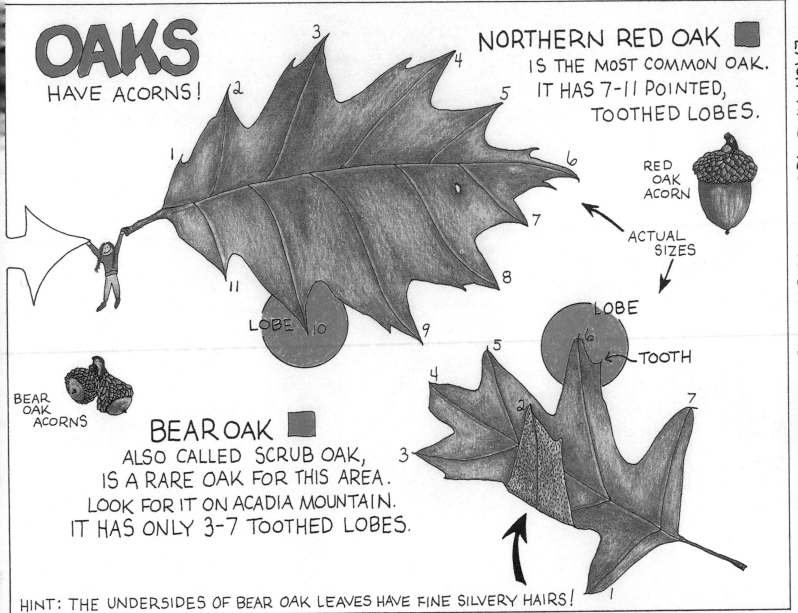

OAKS
HAVE ACORNS!

NORTHERN RED OAK ◼
IS THE MOST COMMON OAK.
IT HAS 7-11 POINTED,
TOOTHED LOBES.

RED OAK ACORN

ACTUAL SIZES

LOBE

TOOTH

BEAR OAK ACORNS

BEAR OAK ◼
ALSO CALLED SCRUB OAK,
IS A RARE OAK FOR THIS AREA.
LOOK FOR IT ON ACADIA MOUNTAIN.
IT HAS ONLY 3-7 TOOTHED LOBES.

LOBE

HINT: THE UNDERSIDES OF BEAR OAK LEAVES HAVE FINE SILVERY HAIRS!

EACH TIME YOU FIND A NEW TREE PUT A ✓ IN THE ◼!

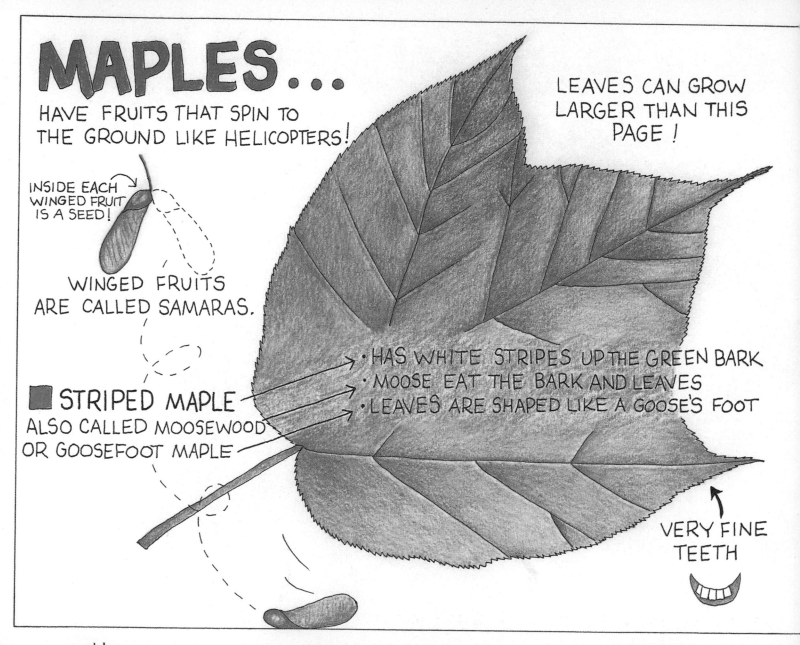

MAPLES...

HAVE FRUITS THAT SPIN TO THE GROUND LIKE HELICOPTERS!

INSIDE EACH WINGED FRUIT IS A SEED!

WINGED FRUITS ARE CALLED SAMARAS.

LEAVES CAN GROW LARGER THAN THIS PAGE!

■ STRIPED MAPLE
ALSO CALLED MOOSEWOOD OR GOOSEFOOT MAPLE

• HAS WHITE STRIPES UP THE GREEN BARK
• MOOSE EAT THE BARK AND LEAVES
• LEAVES ARE SHAPED LIKE A GOOSE'S FOOT

VERY FINE TEETH

...AND MORE MAPLES

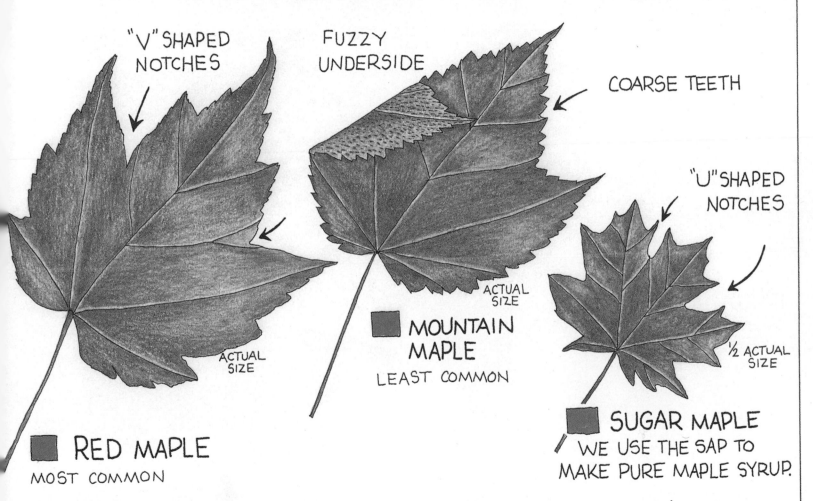

"V" SHAPED NOTCHES

FUZZY UNDERSIDE

COARSE TEETH

"U" SHAPED NOTCHES

ACTUAL SIZE

MOUNTAIN MAPLE

LEAST COMMON

½ ACTUAL SIZE

RED MAPLE

MOST COMMON

SUGAR MAPLE
WE USE THE SAP TO MAKE PURE MAPLE SYRUP.

DON'T TURN THE PAGE UNLESS YOU'RE READY FOR A QUESTION ABOUT MAPLES!

HERE IS A TRICKY QUESTION! READY?

HOW MANY DIFFERENT KINDS OF MAPLE LEAVES ARE ON THESE TWO PAGES?

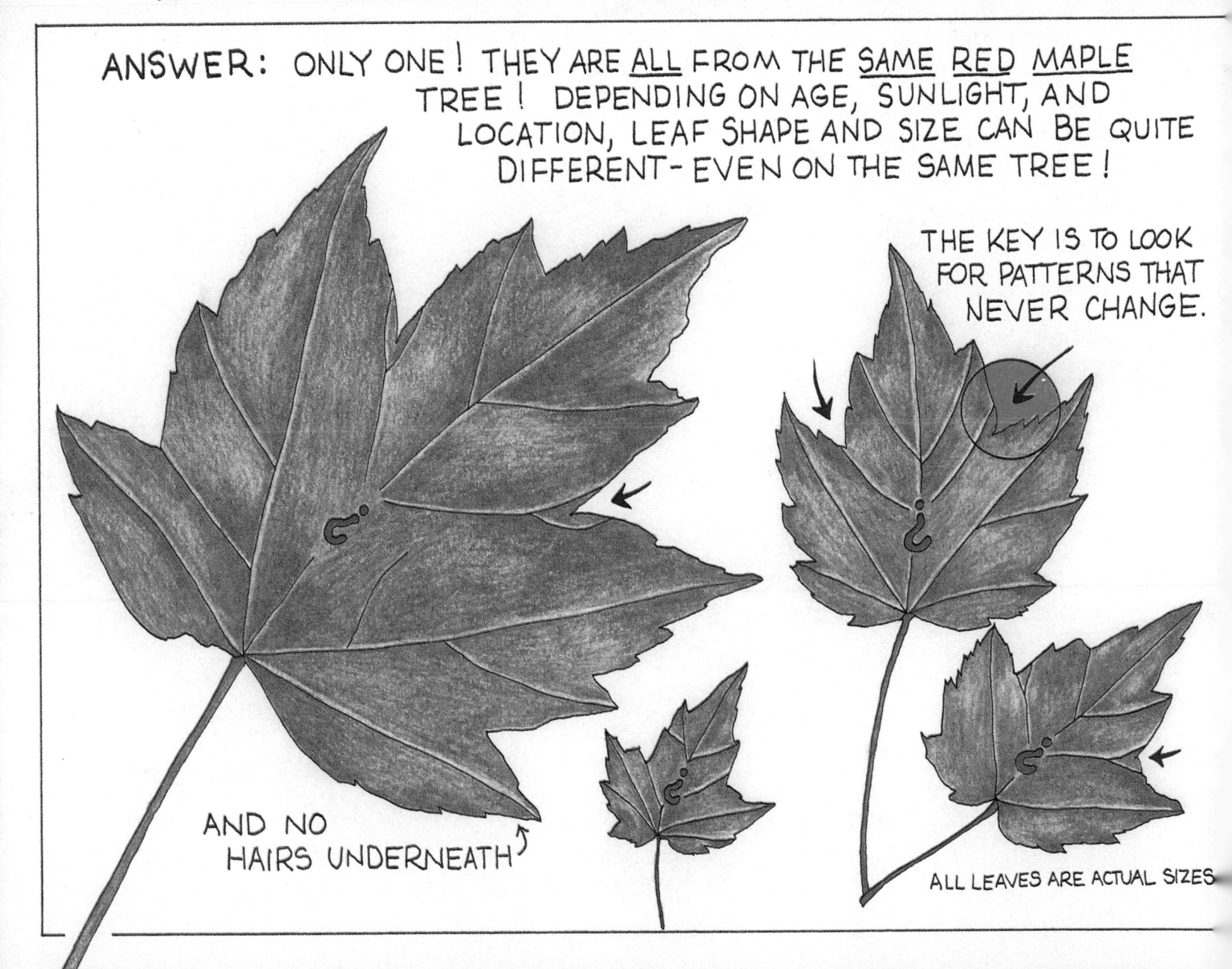

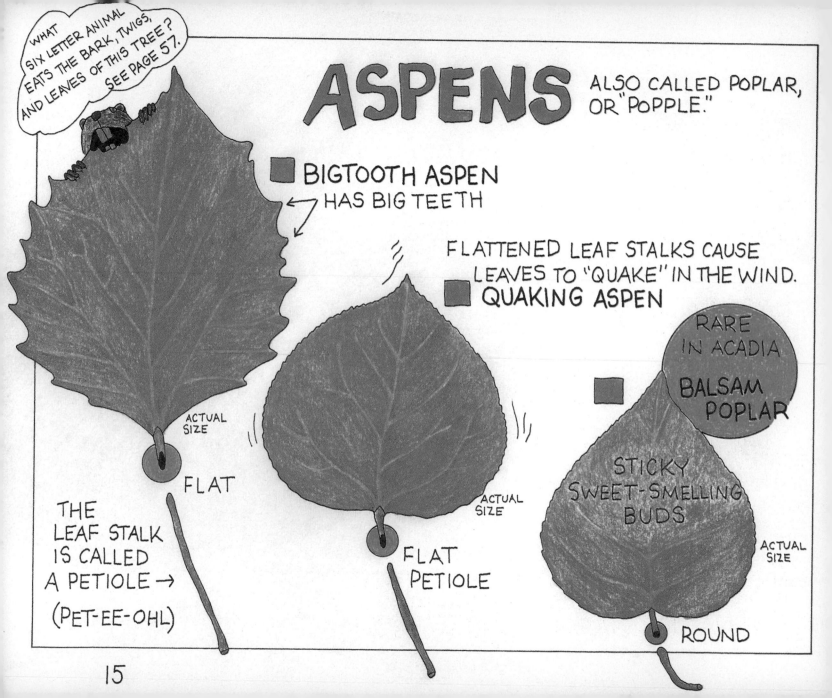

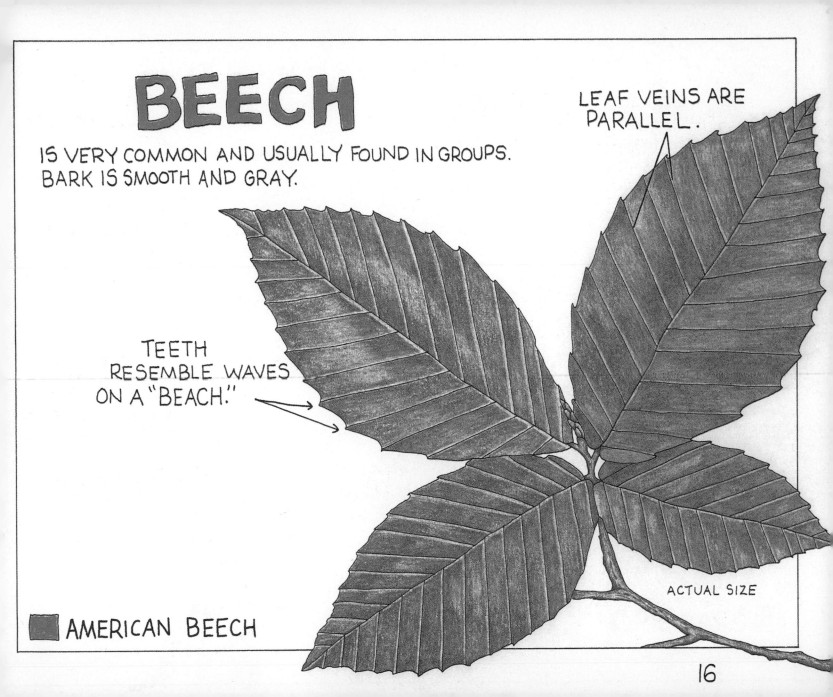

BEECH

IS VERY COMMON AND USUALLY FOUND IN GROUPS.
BARK IS SMOOTH AND GRAY.

LEAF VEINS ARE PARALLEL.

TEETH RESEMBLE WAVES ON A "BEACH."

ACTUAL SIZE

AMERICAN BEECH

16

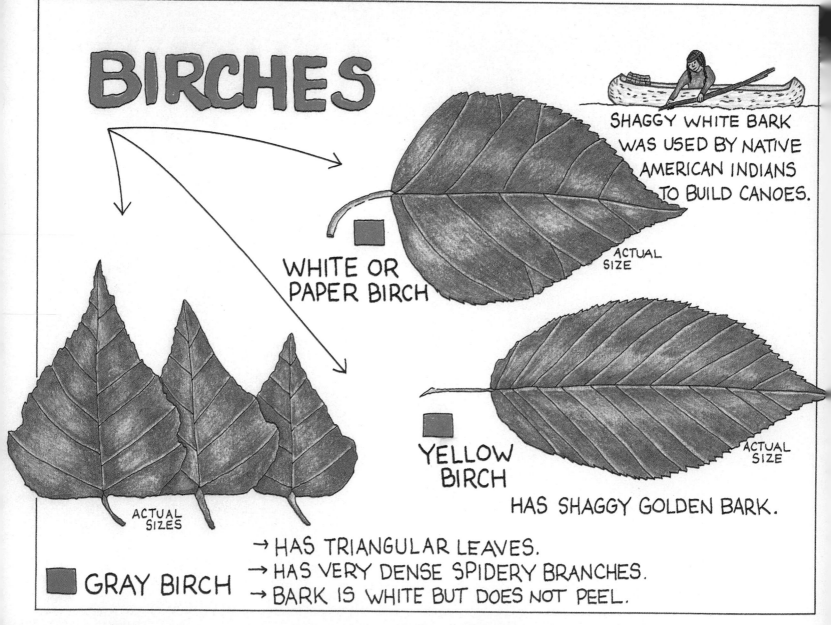

BIRCHES

WHITE OR PAPER BIRCH

SHAGGY WHITE BARK WAS USED BY NATIVE AMERICAN INDIANS TO BUILD CANOES.

ACTUAL SIZE

YELLOW BIRCH

ACTUAL SIZE

HAS SHAGGY GOLDEN BARK.

ACTUAL SIZES

GRAY BIRCH
→ HAS TRIANGULAR LEAVES.
→ HAS VERY DENSE SPIDERY BRANCHES.
→ BARK IS WHITE BUT DOES NOT PEEL.

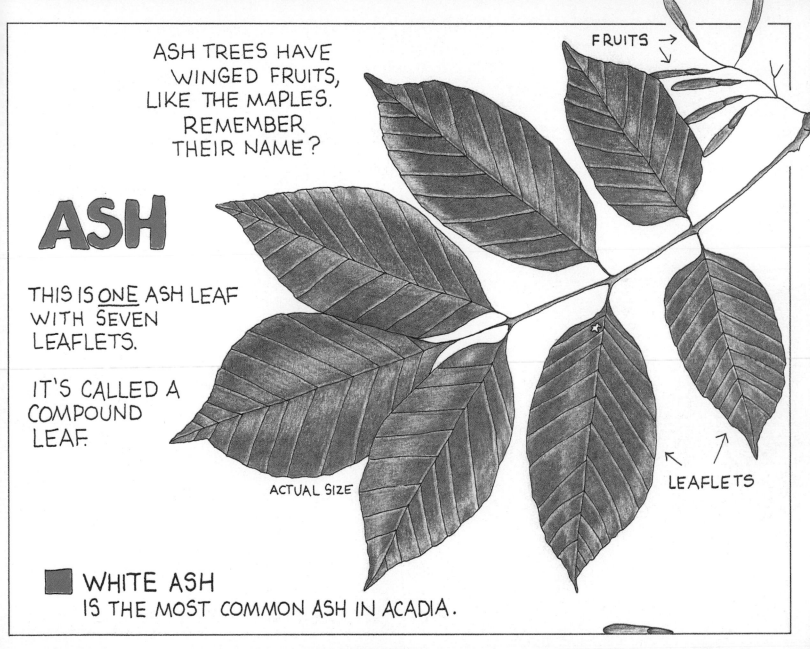

ASH TREES HAVE WINGED FRUITS, LIKE THE MAPLES. REMEMBER THEIR NAME?

ASH

THIS IS <u>ONE</u> ASH LEAF WITH SEVEN LEAFLETS.

IT'S CALLED A COMPOUND LEAF.

ACTUAL SIZE

FRUITS →

LEAFLETS

■ WHITE ASH IS THE MOST COMMON ASH IN ACADIA.

CONIFERS

CONIFERS HAVE CONES

HOW MANY DIFFERENT KINDS OF CONIFEROUS TREES GROW IN ACADIA?

SIX

SPRUCE · PINE · FIR · HEMLOCK · CEDAR
TAMARACK

SOMETIMES CONIFERS ARE CALLED **EVERGREENS** BECAUSE THEY NEVER LOSE ALL THEIR NEEDLES (ACTUALLY LEAVES) AT THE SAME TIME. THEY ARE ALWAYS GREEN, OR "EVERGREEN!"

SCALES

EVERY CONE IS MADE OF LOTS OF SCALES.

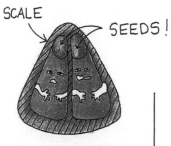

SCALE

SEEDS!

INSIDE EVERY SCALE ARE TWO NAKED (UNPROTECTED) SEEDS.

SUNNY DAYS

CONES OPEN AND SEEDS FLY TO THE GROUND.

RAINY DAYS

CONES CLOSE UNTIL IT'S DRY ENOUGH FOR SEEDS TO FLY!

P.S. IT WON'T BE LONG BEFORE YOU'LL KNOW WHICH TREE IS THE ONE TREE →

LOOK FOR ME HERE TOO!

SPRUCES

HAVE SHARP, SQUARE NEEDLES

SHARP
SQUARE

RED SPRUCE

 MOST COMMON

ACTUAL SIZE

SCALES HAVE A WAVY ROUNDED EDGE.
• BARK IS VERY SCALY.
• NEEDLES ARE A SHINY DARK GREEN COLOR.

WHITE SPRUCE

2ND MOST COMMON

ACTUAL SIZE

SCALES HAVE A SMOOTH FLATTISH EDGE.
• BARK IS SMOOTH WHEN YOUNG, AND SCALY WHEN OLD.
• NEEDLES ARE WHITISH GREEN, AND SMELL LIKE A SKUNK WHEN CRUSHED.

BLACK SPRUCE   FOUND MOSTLY IN BOGS

LEAST COMMON

ACTUAL SIZE

SCALES ARE SMALL AND HAVE A WAVY ROUNDED EDGE.
• CONES USUALLY STAY ON THE TREES FOR MANY YEARS.
• NEEDLES ARE SHORTER AND LESS SHARP THAN OTHER SPRUCES.

IN ACADIA THAT GROWS CONES IN AN UPRIGHT  POSITION! IF YOU CAN FIND ITS TRICKY CONES! HEE! HEE!

DON'T FORGET TO PUT A ✓ IN THE ■ .

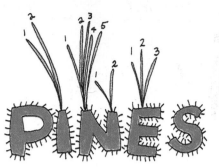

PINES

HAVE NEEDLES THAT GROW IN BUNDLES.

THE WHITE PINE IS MAINE'S STATE TREE. IT HAS THE LARGEST CONES OF ALL THE NEW ENGLAND PINES.

ACTUAL SIZES

BARK HAS SCALY PLATES WITH RED HIGHLIGHTS. NEEDLES ARE VERY LONG.

W H I T E
1 2 3 4 5

ACTUAL SIZES

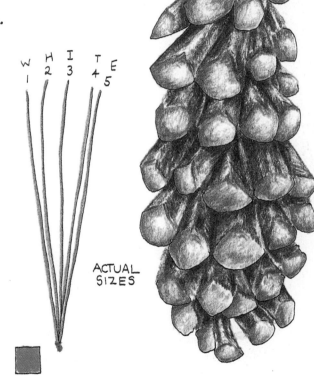

RED PINE

WHITE PINE

IN THE 1700'S, THE BRITISH ROYAL NAVY USED THEM FOR SHIPS' MASTS.

↑ TALLEST PINES IN ACADIA ↑

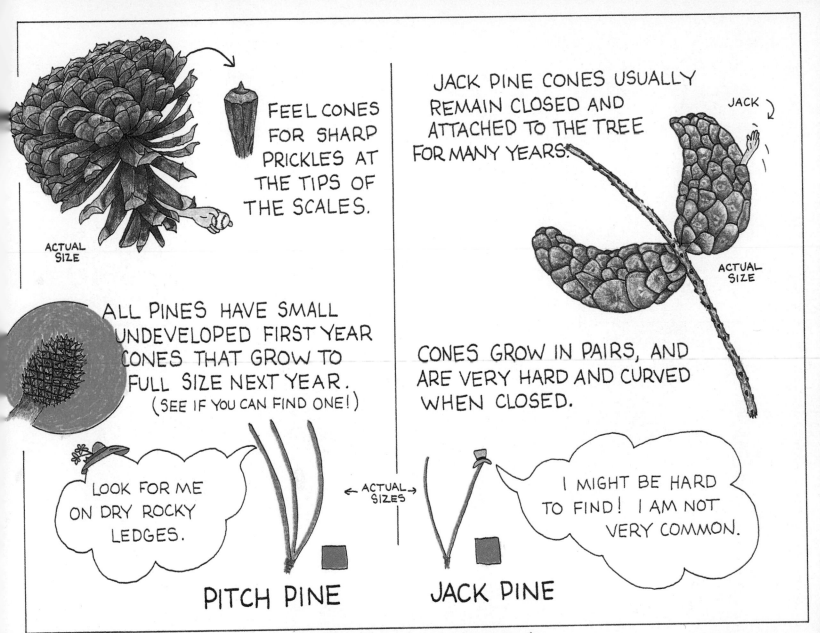

FEEL CONES FOR SHARP PRICKLES AT THE TIPS OF THE SCALES.

ACTUAL SIZE

JACK PINE CONES USUALLY REMAIN CLOSED AND ATTACHED TO THE TREE FOR MANY YEARS.

JACK

ACTUAL SIZE

ALL PINES HAVE SMALL UNDEVELOPED FIRST YEAR CONES THAT GROW TO FULL SIZE NEXT YEAR. (SEE IF YOU CAN FIND ONE!)

CONES GROW IN PAIRS, AND ARE VERY HARD AND CURVED WHEN CLOSED.

LOOK FOR ME ON DRY ROCKY LEDGES.

← ACTUAL SIZES →

I MIGHT BE HARD TO FIND! I AM NOT VERY COMMON.

PITCH PINE

JACK PINE

↖ SHORT SCRAGGILY PINES ↗

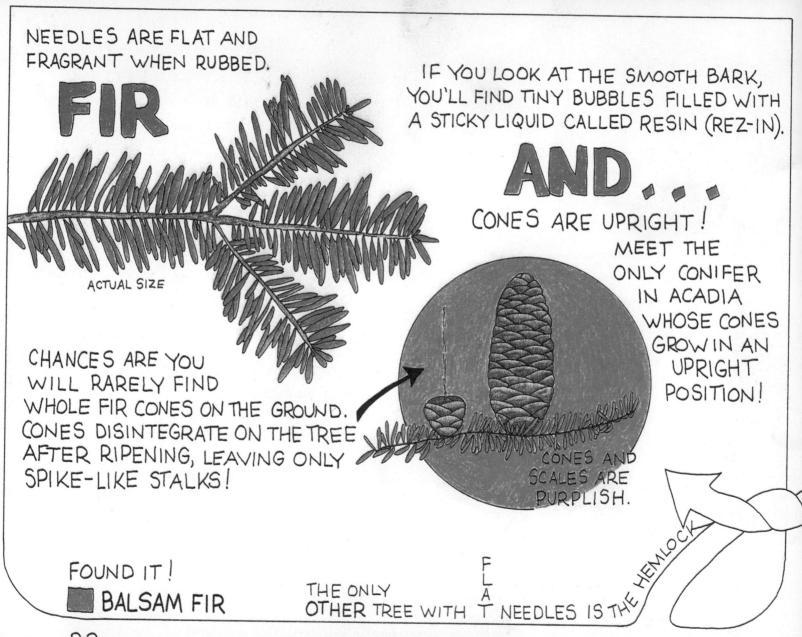

NEEDLES ARE FLAT AND FRAGRANT WHEN RUBBED.

FIR

ACTUAL SIZE

CHANCES ARE YOU WILL RARELY FIND WHOLE FIR CONES ON THE GROUND. CONES DISINTEGRATE ON THE TREE AFTER RIPENING, LEAVING ONLY SPIKE-LIKE STALKS!

IF YOU LOOK AT THE SMOOTH BARK, YOU'LL FIND TINY BUBBLES FILLED WITH A STICKY LIQUID CALLED RESIN (REZ-IN).

AND...

CONES ARE UPRIGHT!

MEET THE ONLY CONIFER IN ACADIA WHOSE CONES GROW IN AN UPRIGHT POSITION!

CONES AND SCALES ARE PURPLISH.

FOUND IT!
■ BALSAM FIR

THE ONLY OTHER TREE WITH FLAT NEEDLES IS THE HEMLOCK

23

THE EASTERN HEMLOCK PREFERS COOL MOIST SOIL. BE SURE TO LOOK NEXT TO STREAMS FOR THIS THIRSTY ONE!

MORE THIRSTY TREES ON THE NEXT PAGES

CONES GROW AT THE ENDS OF BRANCHES.

HEMLOCK

HAS SHORT FLAT NEEDLES.

ACTUAL SIZE

← CLOSED CONE

HEMLOCKS GROW SLOWLY, BUT CAN GET VERY LARGE. CAN YOU REACH ALL THE WAY AROUND THE TREE YOU FOUND?

 EASTERN HEMLOCK

THE ONLY OTHER TREE WITH FLAT NEEDLES IS THE FIR. HEMLOCK NEEDLES ARE SHORTER.

LOOK CAREFULLY FOR THE SMALL INCONSPICUOUS CONES OF THE WHITE CEDAR.

I GROW IN SWAMPS, ALONG STREAMS AND IN MOIST SOIL.

SCALE-LIKE LEAVES LOOK AS IF THEY'VE BEEN PRESSED IN A BOOK.

CEDAR

ALSO CALLED ARBOR VITAE (AR-BER VI-TEE), WHICH IS LATIN FOR "TREE OF LIFE."

ACTUAL SIZE

ARE THE LOWER BRANCHES OF YOUR CEDAR NIBBLED? HAS A DEER BEEN THERE BEFORE YOU? THE DEER ON PAGE 59 KNOWS!

I'M A PRO!
NORTHERN WHITE CEDAR

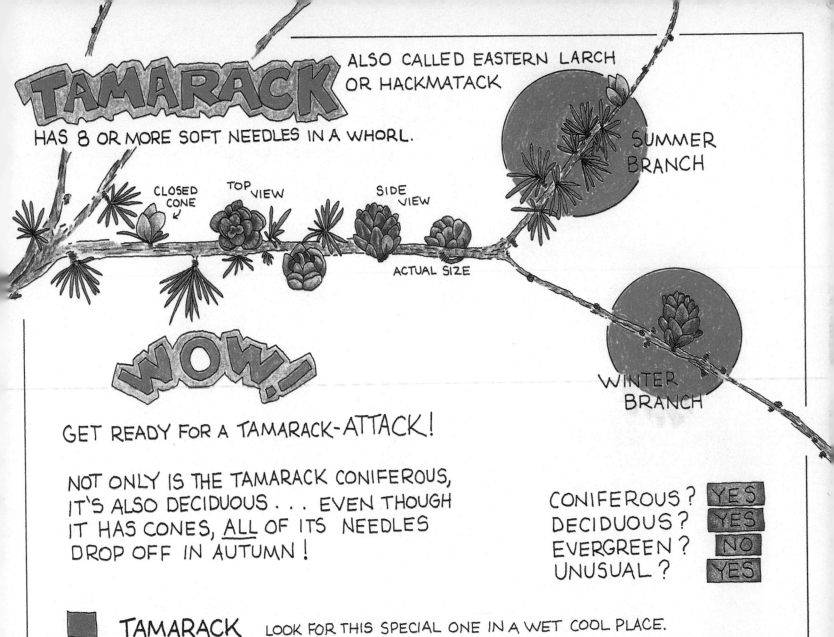

TAMARACK

ALSO CALLED EASTERN LARCH OR HACKMATACK

HAS 8 OR MORE SOFT NEEDLES IN A WHORL.

SUMMER BRANCH

CLOSED CONE

TOP VIEW

SIDE VIEW

ACTUAL SIZE

WINTER BRANCH

WOW!

GET READY FOR A TAMARACK-ATTACK!

NOT ONLY IS THE TAMARACK CONIFEROUS, IT'S ALSO DECIDUOUS . . . EVEN THOUGH IT HAS CONES, ALL OF ITS NEEDLES DROP OFF IN AUTUMN!

CONIFEROUS? YES
DECIDUOUS? YES
EVERGREEN? NO
UNUSUAL? YES

 TAMARACK   LOOK FOR THIS SPECIAL ONE IN A WET COOL PLACE.

26

TREE STUMPERS

ACROSS

2. SPRUCE NEEDLES ARE SHARP AND _____.
3. _____ TREES HAVE CONES.
6. WHICH PINE IS MAINE'S STATE TREE?
7. _____ HAVE NEEDLES THAT LOOK LIKE THEY'VE BEEN PRESSED IN A BOOK.
10. LEAF STALKS ARE ALSO CALLED _____.
12. THE _____ GROW CONES ON THE TIPS OF THEIR BRANCHES ONLY.
14. CONES ARE MADE UP OF MANY _____.
18. THE SAP OF THE _____ MAPLE IS COMMONLY USED TO MAKE MAPLE SYRUP.
19. _____ HAVE FLAT, FRAGRANT, AND "FRIENDLY" NEEDLES.
21. NAME THE DECIDUOUS CONIFER OF ACADIA.
22. WHITE _____ NEEDLES CAN SMELL SKUNK-LIKE.
23. "GREAT OAKS FROM LITTLE _____ GROW."
24. THE CONIFER WHOSE NEEDLES GROW IN BUNDLES
25. LOOK ON ACADIA MTN. FOR _____ OAK.
26. _____ TREES DROP THEIR LEAVES IN THE FALL.

DOWN

1. _____-LEAVED TREES ARE ANOTHER NAME FOR DECIDUOUS TREES.
2. WHAT DO YOU FIND INSIDE THE CONES OF EVERGREENS?
3. A CONE _____ IN THE RAIN.
4. _____ _____ PROTECT PLANTS, WILDLIFE, AND BEAUTIFUL SCENERY.
5. TREES THAT ARE GREEN YEAR-ROUND ARE _____.
6. THE BARK OF THE _____ BIRCH WAS USED BY INDIANS FOR MAKING CANOES.
8. WHICH SPRUCE HAS VERY SCALY BARK?
9. THIS TREE IS A FAVORITE FOOD OF BEAVERS.
10. WHICH PINE HAS 3 NEEDLES IN A BUNDLE?
11. ANOTHER NAME FOR TAMARACK
13. _____ LIKE TO EAT CONIFER SEEDS.
15. THE BEAUTIFUL NAME FOR WINGED SEEDS
16. CONES OF THE _____ TREE BREAK APART BEFORE FALLING TO THE GROUND.
17. LEAVES OF _____ ASPEN "TREMBLE" IN THE SLIGHTEST BREEZE.
20. _____ HAVE SEEDS THAT SPIN LIKE HELICOPTERS.

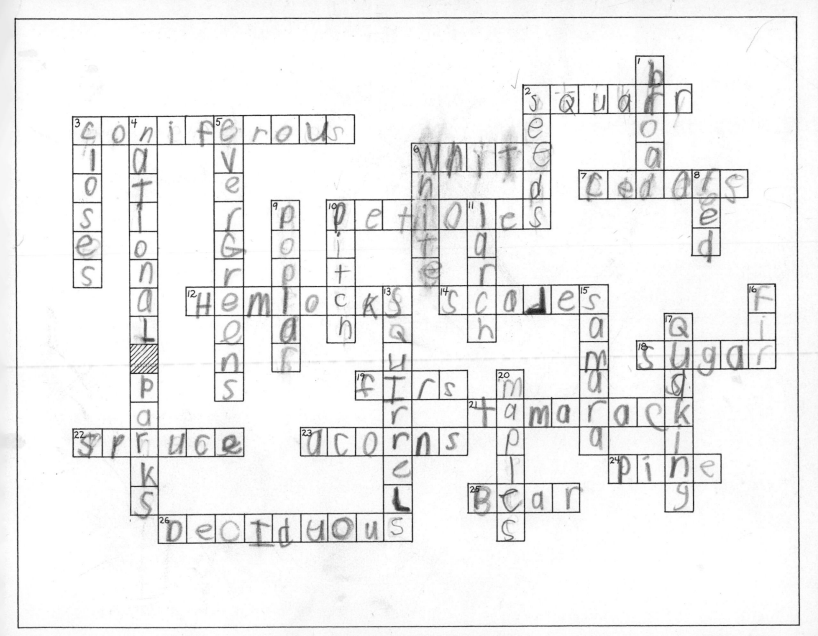

NOTES

2

TEN TANTALIZING TIDEPOOL TALES

- TIDEPOOL LIFE IS EASIEST TO EXPLORE AT LOW TIDE; CHECK THE NEWSPAPER OR RADIO FOR THE TIME.
- PLANTS DIE IF YOU PICK THEM - PLEASE DON'T.
- ANIMALS DIE IF THEY'RE OUT OF COLD WATER TOO LONG. RETURN ALL CRITTERS TO THE EXACT SPOT YOU FOUND THEM.
- USE PAGE 45 TO REMEMBER YOUR FUN DISCOVERIES!

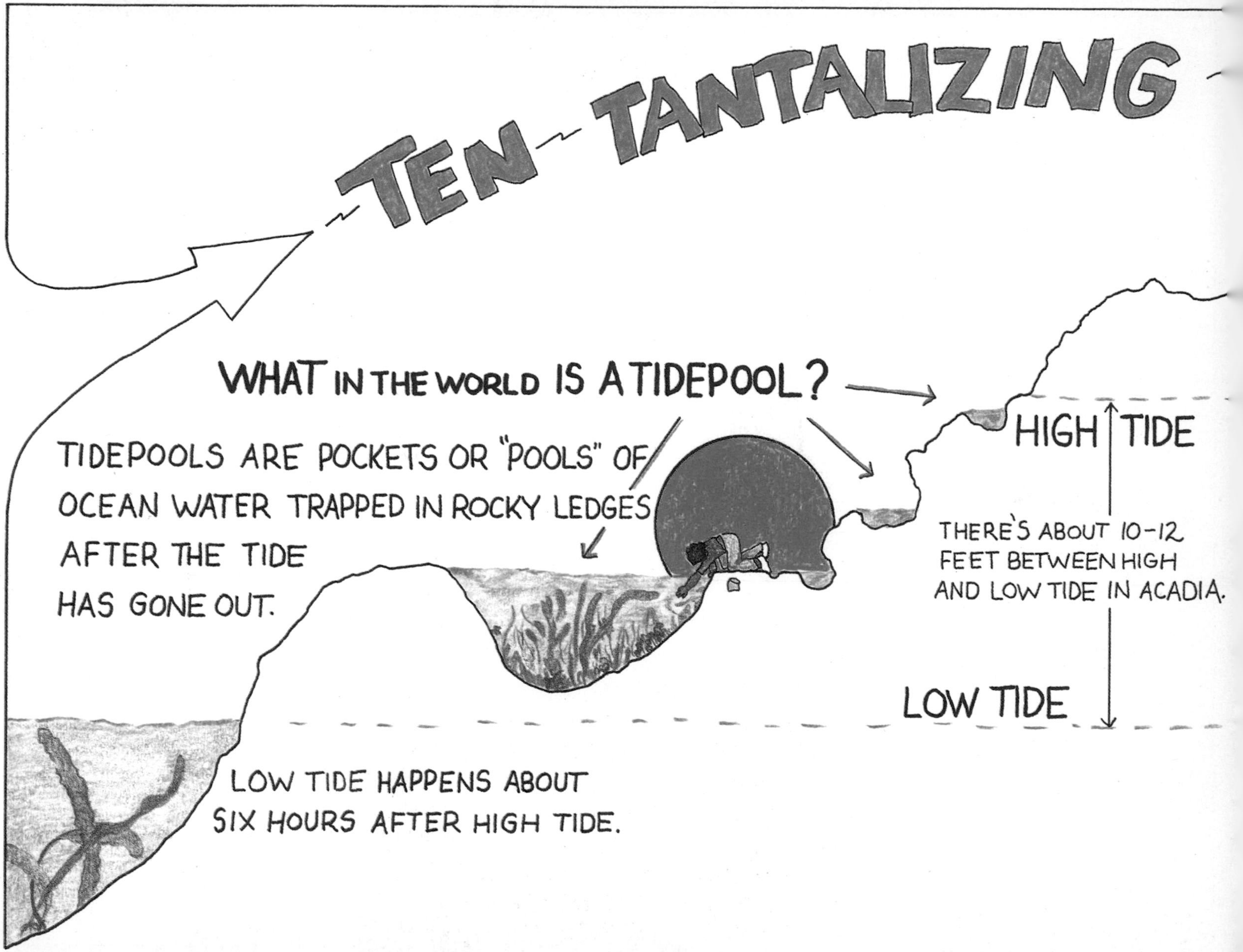

TEN TANTALIZING

WHAT IN THE WORLD IS A TIDEPOOL?

TIDEPOOLS ARE POCKETS OR "POOLS" OF OCEAN WATER TRAPPED IN ROCKY LEDGES AFTER THE TIDE HAS GONE OUT.

HIGH TIDE

THERE'S ABOUT 10-12 FEET BETWEEN HIGH AND LOW TIDE IN ACADIA.

LOW TIDE

LOW TIDE HAPPENS ABOUT SIX HOURS AFTER HIGH TIDE.

TIDEPOOL TALES!

SEASHORE ANIMALS
BEHAVE MOST NATURALLY
<u>UNDER</u> WATER..

BY PUTTING A SEASHORE CREATURE
IN A CLEAR PLASTIC CONTAINER
FILLED WITH COLD SEA WATER, YOU CAN
WATCH —FROM ALL SIDES (EVEN UNDER-
NEATH!)— HOW EACH CRITTER
MOVES, EATS, OPENS AND CLOSES,
AND EXPLORES ITS SURROUNDINGS.

DON'T FALL IN! ROCKS ARE
SLIPPERY AT LOW TIDE!

TALE ONE

BARNACLES, (BAR-NA-KULS)

THAT'S US! WE ARE ONE OF THE FIRST THINGS YOU WILL STEP ON WHILE LOOKING FOR A TIDEPOOL. OUR SHELLS ARE GRAYISH-WHITE WITH SHARP EDGES, AND WE CEMENT OURSELVES PERMANENTLY TO ROCKS. PLEASE, WALK GENTLY OR WE'LL BE CRUSHED.

IF YOU WANT TO MEET US IN PERSON, LOOK IN A TIDEPOOL WHERE WE'LL BE UNDER WATER. IF WE'RE NOT "OUT" WHEN YOU ARRIVE, SWISH THE WATER AROUND US WITH YOUR HAND FOR A FEW SECONDS, THEN WAIT. WE'LL BE OUT TO EAT THE PLANKTON (MICROSCOPIC FOOD) THAT YOU HAVE STIRRED UP!

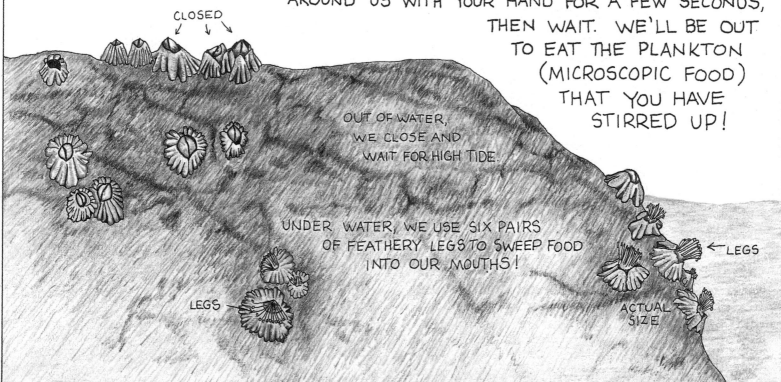

CLOSED

OUT OF WATER, WE CLOSE AND WAIT FOR HIGH TIDE.

UNDER WATER, WE USE SIX PAIRS OF FEATHERY LEGS TO SWEEP FOOD INTO OUR MOUTHS!

LEGS

← LEGS

ACTUAL SIZE

DID YOU LIKE THE BARNACLES? WELL, WE LOVE BARNACLES. IN FACT, WE EAT THEM! WE ARE THE DOG WHELKS, THE CARNIVOROUS (MEAT-EATING) SNAILS OF THE TIDEPOOLS. OUR DRILL-LIKE TONGUE, CALLED A RADULA (RAD-YOU-LA), LETS US BORE THROUGH SHELLS OF THE ANIMALS WE LIKE TO EAT!

DOG WHELKS

OUR SHELLS COME IN MANY COLORS AND PATTERNS. WHAT COLORS CAN YOU FIND?

RECOGNIZE US BY OUR ELLIPTICAL OPENING.

OUR EMPTY SHELLS ARE USED BY HERMIT CRABS.

ACTUAL SIZE

OUR EGG CASES LOOK LIKE RICE GRAINS.

BARNACLES MAKE A TASTY LUNCH! AND DESSERT IS ON PAGE 35!

34

WAIT! BEFORE YOU REACH IN AND STIR UP THE WATER, LOOK FOR US, THE

MUSSELS.

WE FEED ON PLANKTON, LIKE BARNACLES, BUT USE SIPHONS TO FILTER OUR FOOD FROM THE WATER. WE'RE CALLED FILTER FEEDERS.

ACTUAL SIZES

OXYGEN AND PLANKTON GO IN SIPHON #1

AS LONG AS WE ARE UNDER WATER AND NOT DISTURBED, YOU CAN WATCH US FEEDING THROUGH OUR TWO SIPHON OPENINGS. IF YOU TOUCH US OR TAKE US OUT OF WATER, WE'LL CLOSE UP TIGHT.

DEAD MUSSEL

WASTE COMES OUT SIPHON #2

DOG WHELK HOLE!

UNDER CRASHING WAVES, OUR STRONG BYSSAL (BIS-ALL) THREADS HOLD US IN PLACE.

... AND GUESS WHO ELSE EATS MUSSELS? ↑

SEA STARS EAT MUSSELS TOO!

ONCE WE WRAP OUR ARMS AROUND A MUSSEL, WE
USE ALL OF OUR TUBE FEET TO PULL AND PULL
UNTIL ITS SHELL OPENS JUST A LITTLE. THEN,
OUR JELLY-LIKE STOMACH COMES OUT OF OUR
MOUTH (GOOD THING IT'S ON OUR BOTTOM SIDE!)
AND SQUEEZES INTO THE MUSSEL'S SHELL
FOR DINNER. IT'S LIKE EATING "OUT"
EVERY DAY!

PURPLE
SEA
STAR

TUBE
FEET

SEASTAR
EATING A
MUSSEL

BLOOD SEA STARS ARE LITTLE, BRIGHT RED, AND THEIR TURNED UP TIPS SHOW OFF A YELLOW UNDERSIDE.

OUR BIG SPOT ON TOP IS CALLED A
MADREPORITE (MAD-RA-POR-ITE).
THIS OPENING LETS WATER IN AND OUT
OF OUR TUBE FEET SO WE CAN
MOVE AROUND.

ACTUAL SIZES

36

TAKE A BREAK! TIME FOR A

SEA SNACK!

"YUK!" YOU SAY? "WHO WOULD EAT SEAWEED?" LOTS OF PEOPLE! WELL, IT
MAY TAKE SOME GETTING USED TO, BUT GO ON — TRY ME! YOU MIGHT LIKE ME!

DULSE

IS MY NAME. I'M JUST ONE OF <u>MANY</u>
EDIBLE SEAWEEDS. FIND ME AT THE LOW WATER
LINE; I'M REDDISH-PURPLE IN COLOR. EAT A
LITTLE OF ME RIGHT OUT OF
THE OCEAN, OR DRY ME
OUT FIRST IN THE SUN.

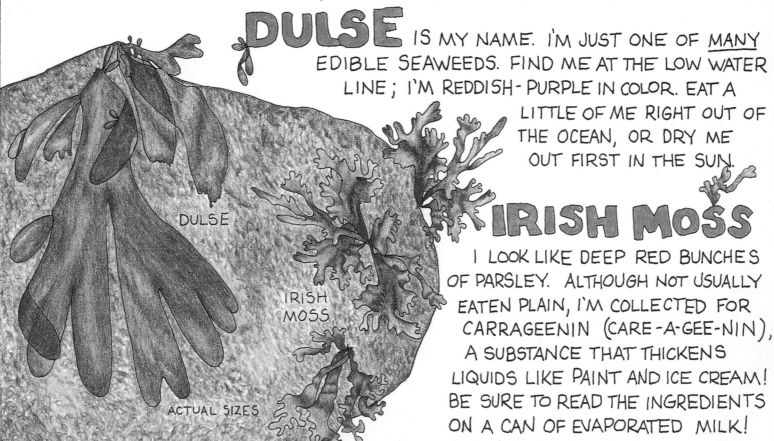

DULSE

IRISH
MOSS

ACTUAL SIZES

IRISH MOSS

I LOOK LIKE DEEP RED BUNCHES
OF PARSLEY. ALTHOUGH NOT USUALLY
EATEN PLAIN, I'M COLLECTED FOR
CARRAGEENIN (CARE-A-GEE-NIN),
A SUBSTANCE THAT THICKENS
LIQUIDS LIKE PAINT AND ICE CREAM!
BE SURE TO READ THE INGREDIENTS
ON A CAN OF EVAPORATED MILK!

WITH SO MANY SPINES, WE CAN LOOK PRETTY MEAN! WE ARE THE GREEN

SEA URCHINS.

OF COURSE WE'RE NOT MEAN! YOU CAN EVEN PICK US UP, IF YOU'RE CAREFUL. ALTHOUGH OUR SPINES AREN'T POISONOUS (LIKE SOME SEA URCHINS IN FLORIDA), THEY ARE VERY SHARP. SO BE GENTLE BUT PERSISTENT, WHILE YOU CONVINCE OUR FEET TO LET GO.

YES! WE HAVE TUBE FEET LIKE OUR COUSINS, THE SEA STARS. WHILE WE'RE UNDER WATER, OUR FEET OFTEN STRETCH OUT BEYOND OUR SPINES, HOLDING US TO ROCKS AND HELPING US TRAVEL.

GULLS LOVE TO EAT OUR INSIDES.

AFTER WE DIE, OUR SHARP SPINES FALL OFF, AND OUR BEAUTIFUL SHELL, CALLED A TEST, IS ALL THAT IS LEFT. AT SAND BEACH, THE SAND INCLUDES MANY BROKEN GREEN SPINES! SEE IF YOU CAN FIND A FEW.

SPINES

TEST

TUBE FEET

LOOK FOR OUR FIVE, WHITE TEETH UNDERNEATH. THEY'RE GREAT FOR EATING SEAWEEDS AND ANIMAL REMAINS.

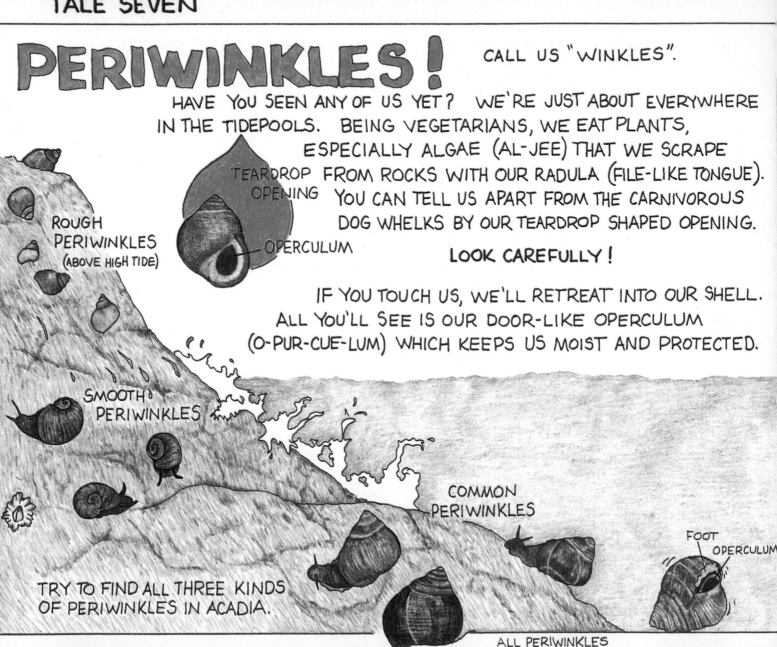

PERIWINKLES!

CALL US "WINKLES".

HAVE YOU SEEN ANY OF US YET? WE'RE JUST ABOUT EVERYWHERE IN THE TIDEPOOLS. BEING VEGETARIANS, WE EAT PLANTS, ESPECIALLY ALGAE (AL-JEE) THAT WE SCRAPE FROM ROCKS WITH OUR RADULA (FILE-LIKE TONGUE). YOU CAN TELL US APART FROM THE CARNIVOROUS DOG WHELKS BY OUR TEARDROP SHAPED OPENING.

LOOK CAREFULLY!

IF YOU TOUCH US, WE'LL RETREAT INTO OUR SHELL. ALL YOU'LL SEE IS OUR DOOR-LIKE OPERCULUM (O-PUR-CUE-LUM) WHICH KEEPS US MOIST AND PROTECTED.

SMALLEST

BIGGER

BIGGEST

ROUGH PERIWINKLES (ABOVE HIGH TIDE)

TEARDROP OPENING

OPERCULUM

SMOOTH PERIWINKLES

COMMON PERIWINKLES

FOOT
OPERCULUM

TRY TO FIND ALL THREE KINDS OF PERIWINKLES IN ACADIA.

ALL PERIWINKLES ARE ACTUAL SIZE.

LIMPETS

ARE VEGETARIAN SNAILS TOO. BECAUSE OF THE SHAPE OF OUR SHELL, WE ARE ALSO CALLED CHINAMAN'S HATS!

WE HAVE ONE SHELL AND NO PROTECTIVE OPERCULUM LIKE THE PERIWINKLES. INSTEAD, OUR "FOOT" ACTS LIKE A SUCTION CUP, HOLDING US TIGHTLY TO ROCKS. THIS KEEPS US FROM DRYING OUT AT LOW TIDE, OR GETTING KNOCKED AROUND AT HIGH TIDE!

IF YOU CAN MANAGE TO SLIDE US FROM OUR ROCK, TURN US OVER AND MEET US IN PERSON! (AND SCOOT US SIDEWAYS; DON'T TRY TO PRY US UP – IT HURTS!)

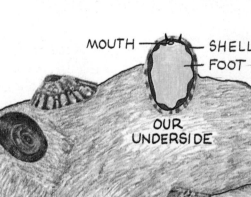

MOUTH — SHELL — FOOT

OUR UNDERSIDE

ACTUAL SIZES

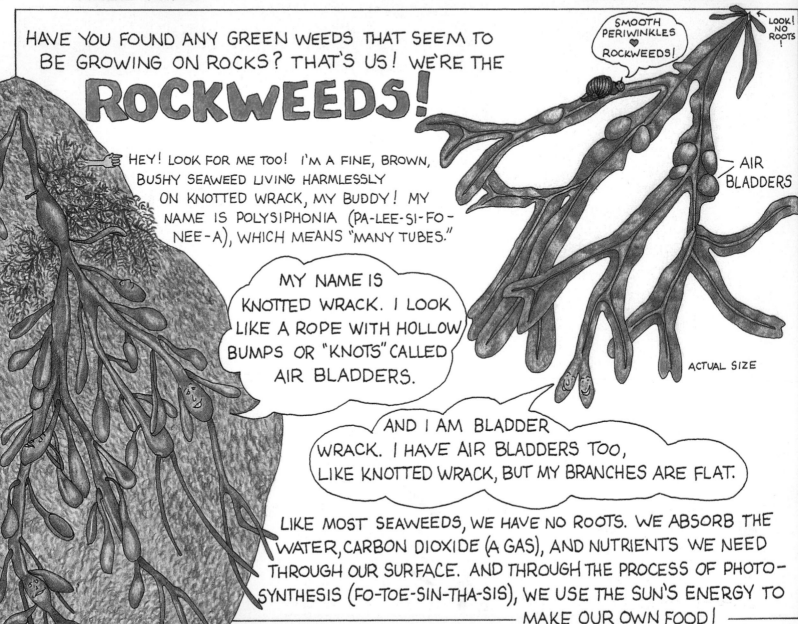

CRABS!

LOOK FOR US UNDER ROCKWEEDS AND BOULDERS, HIDING FROM HUNGRY GULLS!

ROCK CRABS. WE HAVE A SMOOTH-EDGED SHELL.

JONAH CRABS. WE LOOK SIMILAR TO ROCK CRABS, BUT HAVE A ROUGH-EDGED SHELL.

GREEN CRABS.

HERMIT CRABS. WE LIVE IN THE EMPTY SHELLS OF SNAILS AFTER THEY DIE. AS WE GROW, WE LOOK FOR BIGGER SHELLS!

WE'RE ALL SCAVENGERS, EATING WHATEVER WE CAN FIND AS WE WALK SIDE-WAYS ALONG THE OCEAN BOTTOM.

REMEMBER TO PICK US UP FROM THE REAR, FAR FROM OUR CLAWS!

TIDEPOOL TRIVIA

ACROSS

2. _____ CRABS NEED EMPTY SHELLS TO LIVE IN.
4. A SNAIL'S PROTECTIVE "DOOR"
7. WHICH SEAWEED'S NAME MEANS MANY TUBES?
9. SEA _____ EAT BY PUSHING THEIR STOMACH OUT THROUGH THEIR MOUTH.
11. _____ IS A PROCESS WHERE PLANTS MAKE THEIR OWN FOOD USING THE SUN'S ENERGY.
16. A LIMPET'S SHELL RESEMBLES A _____ HAT.
17. SEASTARS' TUBE FEET ARE CONTROLLED BY WATER THAT ENTERS THE _____.
18. TINY PLANTS AND ANIMALS THAT DRIFT IN THE OCEAN
20. A DOG WHELK'S _____ CAN BORE HOLES IN SHELLS.
21. _____ BLANKET ROCKS AT LOW TIDE.
24. _____ ARE CARNIVOROUS SNAILS THAT HAVE ELLIPTICAL OPENINGS.
27. WHICH PERIWINKLE DOES NOT LIKE BEING SUBMERGED AT HIGH TIDE?
28. A SEA urchin HAS FIVE WHITE TEETH.
29. STARFISH AND SEA URCHINS HAVE _____ FEET.
30. THE _____ OF A SEA URCHIN ARE USED FOR PROTECTION AND MOVING AROUND.

DOWN

1. THE SCAVENGERS OF ACADIA'S TIDEPOOLS
3. THE _____ COVERS 3/4 OF THE EARTH'S SURFACE.
5. YOU'LL BE CONVINCED WHEN CRABS ARE NEAR, THAT IT'S ALWAYS BEST TO PICK THEM UP FROM THE _rear_!
6. _____ HOLD TIGHTLY TO ROCKS BY THE SUCTION OF THEIR FOOT.
8. _____ ARE VEGETARIAN SNAILS OF ACADIA.
10. THE LARGEST PERIWINKLE IS THE _____.
12. EVEN THOUGH SEA STARS ARE COMMONLY CALLED _____, THEY ARE NOT RELATED TO FISH.
13. A POCKET OF WATER TRAPPED IN ROCKY LEDGES AFTER THE TIDE HAS GONE OUT
14. A SEA URCHIN'S SHELL IS CALLED A _____.
15. _____ PRODUCE CEMENT THAT HOLDS IN BOTH WET AND DRY CONDITIONS.
19. _____ HOLD TO ROCKS WITH BYSSAL THREADS.
22. _____ PERIWINKLES ARE USUALLY ON ROCKWEEDS.
23. THERE ARE _____ KINDS OF "WINKLES" IN ACADIA.
25. ONE OF MANY EDIBLE SEAWEEDS
26. THE RISE & FALL OF THE OCEAN TWICE A DAY

43

1. C (down) — crab
2. hermit (across)
3. O (down) — ocean
4. operculum (across)
5. sea (down)
6. limpets (down)
7. polysiphonia (across)
8. periwinkles (down)
9. stars (across)
10. romano (down)
11. photosynthesis (across)
12. starfish (down)
13. tide (down)
14. test (down)
15. Barnacles (down)
16. chinamans (across)
17. manreporite (across)
18. plankton (across)
19. mussels (down)
20. radula (across)
21. rockweeds (across)
22. smooth (down)
23. turtle (down)
24. whelks (across)
25. souldes (down)
26. tides (down)
27. rough (across)
28. urchin (across)
29. feet (across)
30. suchse (across)

NOTES

45

3

ANIMAL ADVENTURES

REMEMBER TO:

- bring binoculars (if you have them)
- use page 69 to record your animal observations
- cover a flashlight with red plastic to watch animals at night.

Have a Blast!

ANIMAL

AFTER THE RAIN

IN THE DARK

47

ADVENTURES

DUSK AND DAWN

DURING THE DAY

BEECH MTN

48

IN THE DARK

RACCOONS

ANIMALS THAT ARE ACTIVE AT NIGHT ARE CALLED NOCTURNAL (NOK-TER-NUL) ANIMALS.

LIKE MANY NOCTURNAL ANIMALS, RACCOONS SEE WELL AT NIGHT THANKS TO A MIRROR-LIKE STRUCTURE IN EACH EYE. THIS "MIRROR" REFLECTS AND INTENSIFIES FAINT LIGHT SO RACCOONS CAN SEE BETTER AFTER DARK.

THIS "MIRROR" ALSO CAUSES RACCOONS' EYES TO SHINE YELLOW WHEN THEY ARE CAUGHT BY BEAMS OF HEADLIGHTS OR FLASHLIGHTS AT NIGHT!

RACCOONS MAY EAT INSECTS, FROGS, BERRIES, FISH AND EGGS OF TURTLES AND BIRDS. MANY RACCOONS HAVE ALSO LEARNED TO RAID GARBAGE CANS FOR FOOD!

49

RACCOONS LIVE IN STANDING OR FALLEN HOLLOW TREES CALLED DENS. IF YOU FIND A HOLLOW TREE IN THE DAYTIME, REMEMBER WHERE IT IS. BY QUIETLY RETURNING AT NIGHT, YOU MAY HAVE A CHANCE TO SEE IF THE TREE IS INHABITED!

SIGNS OF RACCOONS

1. TRACKS – USUALLY NEAR STREAMS OR PONDS
2. SILVER-TIPPED HAIRS AROUND HOLES IN TREES WHERE RACCOONS HAVE CLIMBED IN AND OUT
3. TIPPED OVER GARBAGE CANS!

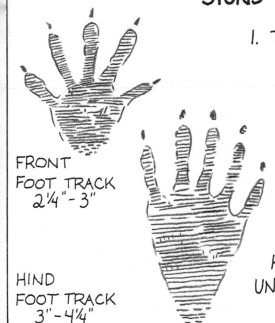

FRONT FOOT TRACK 2¼" - 3"

HIND FOOT TRACK 3" - 4¼"

– CAUTION –

ALTHOUGH RACCOONS ARE CUTE, DON'T TRY TO HAND-FEED THEM. WILD ANIMALS CAN EASILY MIS-UNDERSTAND EVEN A SMALL MOVEMENT AND MIGHT BITE IN STARTLED REACTION.

IN THE DARK
FIREFLIES

FIREFLIES,
OR LIGHTNING BUGS,
ARE INSECTS THAT HAVE
LIGHTS TO SIGNAL EACH OTHER
DURING MATING.

THE MALE FLASHES HIS LIGHT,
THE FEMALE REPLIES WITH HERS!

FIREFLIES OF THE SAME KIND
RECOGNIZE EACH OTHER BY:
    - THE NUMBER OF FLASHES
    - HOW LONG THE LIGHT LASTS
    - THE COLOR OF THE LIGHT
      (YELLOW, BLUE, GREEN...)

HOW MANY KINDS OF FIREFLIES CAN YOU FIND
IN ACADIA? LOOK IN WET AREAS DURING SUMMER NIGHTS.

MALES SIGNAL
WHEN FLYING.

FEMALES SIGNAL
FROM PERCHES NEAR
THE GROUND.

FIREFLIES ARE REALLY BEETLES, NOT FLIES!
HERE'S A TRICK TO RECOGNIZE MOST BEETLES FROM
OTHER INSECTS: LOOK FOR A PAIR OF HARDENED WINGS
THAT MEET IN A STRAIGHT LINE DOWN THE BEETLE'S BACK.
HIDDEN BENEATH IS A PAIR OF DELICATE WINGS USED FOR FLYING.

HARDENED WINGS

DELICATE WINGS

HOW CAN YOU TELL AN INSECT FROM OTHER ANIMALS?

ADULT INSECTS HAVE 3 BODY PARTS
WITH SIX LEGS ATTACHED TO THE
MIDDLE PART.

— HEAD
— THORAX
— ABDOMEN

AFTER FIREFLIES MATE, FEMALES LAY EGGS THAT HATCH INTO LARVAE (LAR-VEE).
A LARVA IS A WORM-LIKE STAGE OF A NEWLY HATCHED
INSECT. THE LARVAE OF FIREFLIES ALSO
GLOW, WHICH IS WHY THEY ARE CALLED GLOWWORMS!
LOOK FOR SMALL DOTS OF LIGHT ON THE GROUND
SEVERAL WEEKS AFTER THE ADULTS STOP THEIR
MATING SIGNALS. (EACH KIND OF FIREFLY MATES DURING A
DIFFERENT TIME OF SUMMER.) IN FALL, LARVAE BURY THEMSELVES
IN SOIL. IN SPRING, THEY EMERGE AND CHANGE TO ADULT FIREFLIES.

2x ACTUAL SIZE

FIREFLY
LARVA
(GLOWWORM)

IS A SPIDER AN INSECT? FIND OUT ON PAGE 53!

AFTER THE RAIN

SPIDERS!

WOW!
HAVE YOU EVER
WATCHED A SPIDER
SPIN ITS WEB OR
EAT A FLY?
IT'S GREAT! YOU CAN
FIND SPIDERS BY FIRST
LOOKING FOR THEIR GLISTENING
WEBS AFTER A LIGHT RAIN.

UNLIKE INSECTS, SPIDERS
HAVE 8 LEGS AND ONLY
2 BODY PARTS. AND ALTHOUGH
MOST SPIDERS HAVE 8 EYES
- YES, EIGHT EYES -
MANY OF THEM HAVE
POOR EYESIGHT!

← DRAGLINE

MALE

IN ACADIA,
THE ORB-WEAVERS
ARE AN EXCITING
GROUP OF SPIDERS
TO WATCH BECAUSE
THEY USUALLY SPIN A
NEW WEB EACH DAY.
THEY GET THEIR NAME
BECAUSE THEY SPIN
CIRCULAR WEBS.
(ORB MEANS ROUND.)

MALE SPIDERS USUALLY
HAVE SMALLER BODIES
AND LONGER LEGS
THAN FEMALES.

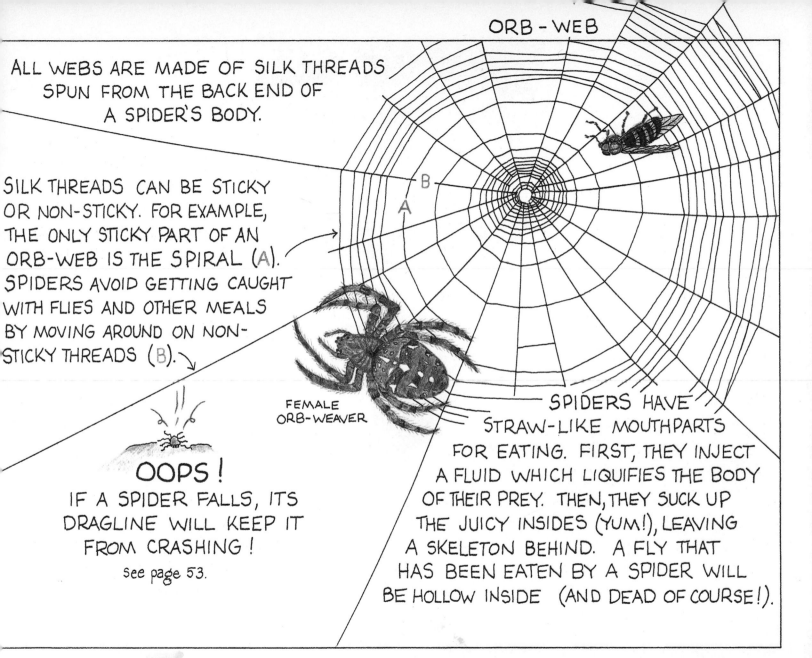

ALL WEBS ARE MADE OF SILK THREADS SPUN FROM THE BACK END OF A SPIDER'S BODY.

SILK THREADS CAN BE STICKY OR NON-STICKY. FOR EXAMPLE, THE ONLY STICKY PART OF AN ORB-WEB IS THE SPIRAL (A). SPIDERS AVOID GETTING CAUGHT WITH FLIES AND OTHER MEALS BY MOVING AROUND ON NON-STICKY THREADS (B).

OOPS!
IF A SPIDER FALLS, ITS DRAGLINE WILL KEEP IT FROM CRASHING!

See page 53.

FEMALE ORB-WEAVER

SPIDERS HAVE STRAW-LIKE MOUTHPARTS FOR EATING. FIRST, THEY INJECT A FLUID WHICH LIQUIFIES THE BODY OF THEIR PREY. THEN, THEY SUCK UP THE JUICY INSIDES (YUM!), LEAVING A SKELETON BEHIND. A FLY THAT HAS BEEN EATEN BY A SPIDER WILL BE HOLLOW INSIDE (AND DEAD OF COURSE!).

54

AFTER THE RAIN

SLUGS

FIND A SLUG AND LOOK CAREFULLY AT ITS BACK. SEE ANYTHING THAT LOOKS LIKE A SADDLE FOR A HORSE? THAT'S THE MANTLE!

SADDLE-LIKE MANTLE

BREATHING HOLE

ON THE RIGHT-HAND SIDE OF A SLUG'S BODY, LOOK FOR A SMALL HOLE AT THE LOWER EDGE OF ITS MANTLE. SLUGS BREATHE THROUGH THIS HOLE! IF YOU CAN'T FIND IT, BE PATIENT; THE HOLE MAY BE TEMPORARILY CLOSED.

DID YOU KNOW THAT SLUGS ARE RELATIVES OF THE PERIWINKLES, LIMPETS, DOG WHELKS, AND MUSSELS? (REMEMBER THEM?) SLUGS, HOWEVER DON'T HAVE SHELLS.

THE LONG PAIR OF TENTACLES ARE FOR "SEEING."

THE SHORT PAIR ARE FOR FEELING.

MOUTH

FOOT

SPECIAL GLANDS IN SLUGS' AND SNAILS' SKIN MAKE A SLIMY JUICE CALLED MUCUS (MEW-KUS). MUCUS KEEPS SLUGS MOIST, PROTECTS THEM FROM SHARP OBJECTS, AND PROVIDES A WET TRAIL SO THEY CAN EASILY MOVE AROUND.

BE BRAVE AND TRY PICKING UP A SLUG. YOU'LL BE GUARANTEED A BETTER VIEW OF HOW SLUGS SLITHER!

BECAUSE THEY DON'T HAVE SHELLS, SLUGS NEED A MOIST ENVIRONMENT (EN-VI-RON-MENT) OR HOME TO SURVIVE. LOOK FOR THEM UNDER LOGS, ON THE BOTTOM SIDE OF LEAVES, OR IN THE OPEN AFTER SUNSET OR AFTER A RAIN. DON'T FORGET TO LOOK UNDER MUSHROOMS—A SLUG'S FAVORITE SNACK!

A GOOD SIGN OF A SLUG IS ITS SHINY TRAIL.

A SLUG'S UNDERSIDE

DUSK AND DAWN
BEAVERS!

EVEN IF YOU'VE NEVER SEEN BEAVERS' TEETH, ALL YOU NEED TO DO IS TAKE ONE LOOK AT A TREE THEY'VE CUT AND YOU'LL KNOW JUST HOW STRONG AND SHARP THEIR TEETH REALLY ARE. A BEAVER CAN CHEW THROUGH A 6 INCH TREE IN ABOUT 15 MINUTES!

BEAVERS CHEW DOWN TREES BECAUSE THEY LIKE TO EAT THE BARK, LEAVES, AND TWIGS. THEY EAT POND PLANTS TOO.

BEAVERS ARE RODENTS, LIKE SQUIRRELS AND MICE. ALL RODENTS HAVE LONG FRONT TEETH CALLED INCISORS (IN-SY-ZORS) THAT GROW THROUGHOUT THEIR LIFETIME. HOWEVER, THEIR TEETH ALWAYS STAY THE SAME LENGTH BECAUSE OF CONTINUOUS WEAR FROM CHEWING!

(THEIR FAVORITE TREE IS THE POPLAR. BUT THEY ALSO LIKE WHITE BIRCH AND MAPLE.)

57

BEAVERS ALSO CUT TREES TO BUILD LODGES AND DAMS. BE SURE TO LOOK FOR THEIR DOME-SHAPED LODGES IN ACADIA'S STREAMS, PONDS, AND LAKES.

THEIR BEAUTIFUL WIDE TAIL IS EXCELLENT FOR SLAPPING WATER TO WARN OTHER BEAVERS OF DANGER. THEY ALSO USE IT AS A RUDDER WHEN SWIMMING, AND FOR BALANCE (LIKE A KICKSTAND) WHEN CHEWING DOWN TREES. BUT THEY NEVER USE IT FOR CARRYING MUD!

PSST! HEAD OUT 2 HOURS BEFORE SUNSET—LISTEN FOR THEIR TAIL SLAP!

FOR YEARS BEAVERS HAVE BEEN TRAPPED FOR THEIR VALUABLE FUR. IN ACADIA NATIONAL PARK, WHERE TRAPPING IS PROHIBITED, BEAVERS ARE PLENTIFUL, AND FUN TO WATCH!

58

DUSK AND DAWN
DEER

HAVE YOU EVER WALKED THROUGH THE WOODS AND ACCIDENTALLY FRIGHTENED A DEER? AS IT RAN AWAY, CAN YOU REMEMBER HOW IT HELD ITS TAIL HIGH IN THE AIR SHOWING THE BRIGHT WHITE UNDERSIDE? NATURALISTS CALL THIS BEHAVIOR "TAIL-FLAGGING" AND BELIEVE IT MAY WARN OTHER DEER OF DANGER.

I'LL BET YOU CAN GUESS WHY ACADIA'S DEER ARE CALLED WHITE-TAILED DEER!

EACH YEAR IN EARLY SPRING, MALE DEER, OR BUCKS, BEGIN GROWING ANTLERS. A FURRY COVERING CALLED VELVET NOURISHES THE ANTLERS WITH BLOOD, HELPING THEM GROW AS MUCH AS ONE INCH A DAY!

BY THE END OF AUGUST ANTLERS STOP GROWING AND THE DEER RUB OFF THE NOW USELESS VELVET. IN EARLY SEPTEMBER LOOK FOR "ANTLER RUBS" ON TREES LESS THAN 4" IN DIAMETER.

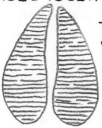

TOES TOGETHER

TRACK OF WALKING DEER

ANTLERS REACH FULL SIZE JUST IN TIME FOR THE AGGRESSIVE, "RUTTING" OR MATING SEASON WHICH LASTS FROM MID-NOVEMBER TO MID-DECEMBER. BUCKS OFTEN USE THEIR ANTLERS WHEN FIGHTING FOR FEMALE DEER, OR DOES (DOZE).

BETWEEN LATE DECEMBER AND LATE JANUARY, BUCKS' ANTLERS FALL OFF. YOU MAY SEE THEM IN THE SNOW, IF RODENTS HAVEN'T EATEN THEM FIRST! (CHECK FOR TINY TOOTHMARKS.)

DEER STAND QUIET AND ALERT — LISTENING, WATCHING, AND SMELLING FOR SIGNS OF DANGER.

TOES
SPREAD

TRACK OF RUNNING DEER

WHEN WINTER FOOD IS SCARCE, DEER WILL EAT LEAVES OF CEDAR TREES.

PAGE 25 WILL HELP YOU RECOGNIZE ACADIA'S CEDARS.

DUSK AND DAWN FROGS

EXCEPT FOR THE WOOD FROG, ACADIA'S FROGS ARE PRIMARILY NOCTURNAL. A SUNSET WALK IS THE PERFECT TIME FOR A FUN GAME CALLED "FROGGING." FIRST, LOCATE FROGS NEAREST YOU BY FOLLOWING THEIR VOICES. WITHOUT LOOKING, GUESS WHICH FROG(S) YOU HEAR USING THE VOICE CLUES ON THE NEXT PAGE. THEN FIND YOUR FROG(S) AND CHECK YOUR GUESS USING THE DRAWINGS. HOW MANY FROGS CAN YOU IDENTIFY USING ONLY YOUR SENSE OF HEARING?

FINDING FROGS IS EASIEST IN SPRING AND EARLY SUMMER WHEN YOU ARE MOST LIKELY TO HEAR THE MATING CALL OF MALE FROGS.

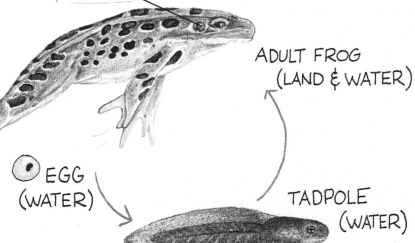

EARDRUM

ADULT FROG (LAND & WATER)

EGG (WATER)

TADPOLE (WATER)

FROGS ARE AMPHIBIANS (AM-FIB-EE-ANNS) AND LIVE A "DOUBLE LIFE"—
—PART ON LAND AND PART IN WATER.

ACADIA'S SIX MOST COMMON FROGS

VOICE: LIKE A LOOSE BANJO STRING

LOOK FOR: TWO RIDGES DOWN THE
BACK

GREEN FROG

VOICE: HIGH-PITCHED, WHISTLE-
LIKE, "PREEP, PREEP, PREEP..."

LOOK FOR: DARK X ON THE BACK

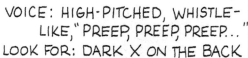

SPRING PEEPER

VOICE: LOW-PITCHED HOARSE SNORE

LOOK FOR: SQUARISH SPOTS ON
THE BACK

PICKEREL FROG

CAUTION: SKIN SECRETES POISON!   WASH HANDS AFTER HANDLING.

VOICE: "JUG-O-RUM" OR "RONK"

LOOK FOR: A RIDGE AROUND EACH
EARDRUM

BULL FROG

LARGEST FROG IN NO. AMERICA

VOICE: SHORT QUACKS OR CLACKS

LOOK FOR: DARK EYE MASK

WOOD FROG

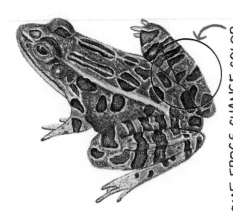

VOICE: DEEP RATTLING SNORE

LOOK FOR: ROUNDISH SPOTS ON BACK

LEOPARD FROG

SOME FROGS CHANGE COLOR
DEPENDING ON TIME OF YEAR.

DURING THE DAY

BALD EAGLES

IMAGINE! EVERY BALD EAGLE GONE FROM THE FACE OF THE EARTH. UNFORTUNATELY THIS IS POSSIBLE! IN THE LAST 50 YEARS, THE BALD EAGLE POPULATION HAS DROPPED SHARPLY. ONE OF THE MAIN CULPRITS IS DDT, A CHEMICAL USED TO KILL INSECTS. WHEN RAIN WASHES DDT INTO RIVERS, LAKES, AND OCEANS, FISH BECOME STOREHOUSES OF THE HARMFUL CHEMICAL. BY EATING FISH, EAGLES ACTUALLY EAT DDT!

DDT REDUCES EAGLES' ABILITY
TO PRODUCE HEALTHY HARD-
SHELLED EGGS. AS A RESULT, EGGS
CAN CRACK BEFORE HATCHING. SINCE
1969, DDT HAS BEEN BANNED IN
THE UNITED STATES, AND ITS EFFECTS
ARE GRADUALLY BEING REDUCED. FINALLY,
EAGLES ARE BEGINNING TO NEST SUCCESS-
FULLY IN MAINE! YIPPEE! BUT BALD EAGLES
ARE STILL ENDANGERED. WHY? HABITAT
DESTRUCTION AND USE OF DDT IN OTHER COUNTRIES
THREATEN EAGLES' SURVIVAL. IT IS IMPORTANT
WE BE CAUTIOUS OF HOW OUR ACTIONS AFFECT
OUR ENVIRONMENT AND OTHER LIVING THINGS.

SINCE EAGLES ARE BIRDS THAT PREY UPON
OR EAT OTHER ANIMALS, THEY ARE KNOWN
AS BIRDS OF PREY. ALL BIRDS OF PREY
HAVE SPECIAL CLAWS CALLED TALONS TO
CAPTURE AND GRIP THEIR FOOD WHILE
EATING. THE BALD EAGLE IS ACADIA'S
LARGEST BIRD OF PREY.

LOOK FOR THEIR HUGE YELLOW BILL. IT HELPS THEM RIP THEIR FOOD INTO PIECES! _____

AN EAGLE'S TALONS

WHAT IS THE
BEST WAY TO SEE
EAGLES IN ACADIA?

- LOOK UP A LOT! LOOK FOR A
  LARGE DARK BODY, A WHITE
  HEAD AND TAIL, AND STRAIGHT
  WINGS WITH A SPAN OF
  ABOUT SIX FEET!
- TAKE A SUMMER BOAT CRUISE.
  EAGLES OFTEN SOAR OVER
  AND FEED NEAR ISLANDS.

CAN YOU NAME TWO OTHER BIRDS OF PREY? SEE CRITTER CROSSWORD!

64

DURING THE DAY

SQUIRRELS

SQUIRRELS!
SQUIRRELS!
SQUIRRELS!

THEY'RE EVERYWHERE!

WANT TO TRY SOME-
THING FUN? FOLLOW ONE
SQUIRREL FOR HALF AN HOUR,
OBSERVING AS MUCH AS YOU CAN.
WHERE DOES IT LIVE? WHAT DOES
IT EAT? HOW DOES IT EAT?
ARE THERE ANY LEFTOVERS?
WHERE DOES IT TAKE FOOD?

ITS BUSHY TAIL CAN BE AN
UMBRELLA IN THE RAIN, AND A
BLANKET WHEN IT'S COLD! CAN
YOU TELL BY TAIL MOVEMENTS IF
YOUR SQUIRREL IS ANGRY, CONTENT,
OR UPSET? YOU CAN USE PAGE 69
TO RECORD YOUR OBSERVATIONS WITH
NOTES AND DRAWINGS. (TAPE RECORDERS
ARE GREAT TO CAPTURE THEIR SOUNDS!)

RED SQUIRREL

IN WINTER, LOOK FOR RED SQUIRRELS' BUSHY EAR TUFTS.

ARE SQUIRRELS RODENTS, LIKE BEAVERS? THIS PICTURE SHOULD GIVE YOU A CLUE! CHECK YOUR ANSWER ON PAGE 57.

SEE IF YOU CAN FIND TWO KINDS OF SQUIRRELS IN ACADIA. RED SQUIRRELS ARE THE MOST COMMON AND LIVE IN CONIFEROUS FORESTS. GRAY SQUIRRELS ARE LARGER AND LIVE IN DECIDUOUS FORESTS. SQUIRRELS ARE ACTIVE EVEN IN WINTER. LOOK FOR THEIR TRACKS IN THE SNOW.

 C = CONIFEROUS TREES = RED SQUIRREL

REMEMBER THESE? →
PAGE 8 MIGHT HELP. **D** = DECIDUOUS TREES = GRAY SQUIRREL

CRITTER CROSSWORD

ACROSS

1. FIREFLIES GLOW DURING THEIR ____ SEASON.
3. SLUGS USE ____ FOR SEEING AND FEELING.
6. SHELL-LESS SNAILS
7. ____ CARRIES BLOOD TO DEER ANTLERS.
10. ANIMALS ACTIVE AT NIGHT ARE ____.
12. ANIMALS WHOSE FRONT TEETH GROW THROUGHOUT THEIR LIFE ARE CALLED ____.
13. DEER ALERT EACH OTHER BY "TAIL-____".
16. SLUGS AND SNAILS PRODUCE ____ TO KEEP THEMSELVES MOIST.
18. A BEAVER'S FAVORITE FOOD
19. ____ HAVE 6 LEGS AND 3 BODY PARTS.
20. WHICH SQUIRREL WOULD YOU BE MOST LIKELY TO FIND IN A SPRUCE TREE?
21. BEAVERS' AND SQUIRRELS' FRONT TEETH ARE CALLED ____.
24. OWLS, HAWKS, AND EAGLES ARE BIRDS OF ____.
26. ____ GROW ANTLERS EVERY YEAR.
27. A FROG HAS A "DOUBLE-LIFE" AND IS AN ____.
29. FROG EGGS HATCH INTO ____.

DOWN

2. EAGLES' CLAWS ARE CALLED ____.
4. ORB-WEAVERS SPIN ____ WEBS.
5. THE ____ FROG IS THE LARGEST IN THE U.S.A.
8. WHEN EVERY ANIMAL OF ONE KIND DIES, THEY BECOME ____.
9. A SPIDER'S SAFETY LINE IS CALLED A ____.
11. ____ ARE ALLOWED TO CUT DOWN TREES IN A NATIONAL PARK.
12. DEER MATE DURING ____ SEASON.
14. THE LARGEST SQUIRREL IN ACADIA
15. THE LARVA OF A FIREFLY
17. A TREE-CLIMBING RODENT
22. SPIDERS SPIN WEBS MADE OF ____.
23. SPIDERS HAVE ____ LEGS.
25. THE PART OF A SLUG'S BACK THAT LOOKS LIKE A HORSE'S SADDLE
26. WHAT KIND OF AN INSECT IS A FIREFLY?
28. AN INSECT POISON THAT COULD DESTROY AN ENTIRE POPULATION OF EAGLES

NOTES

4

THINGS
YOU MAY TAKE
FROM ACADIA

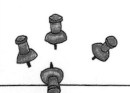

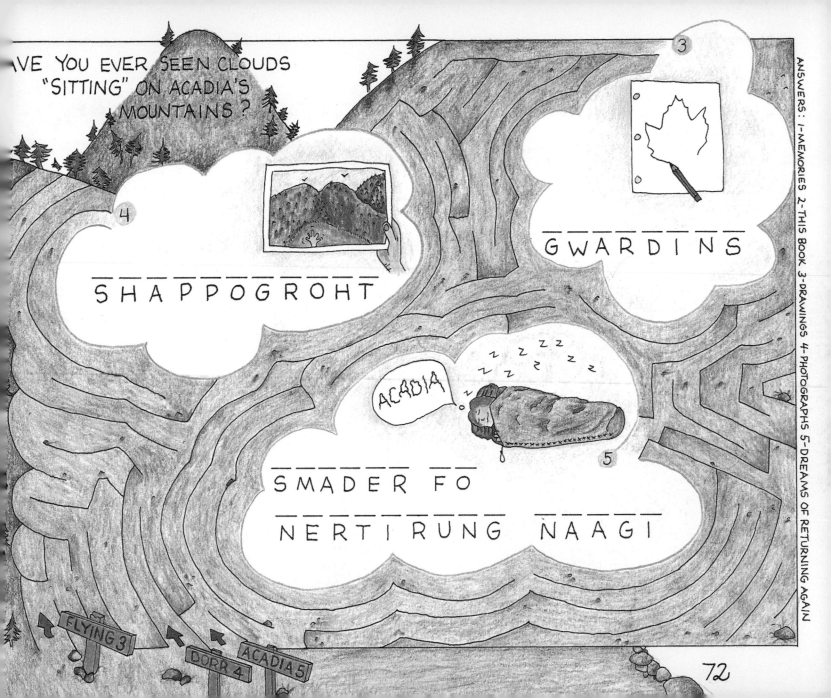

MILLIONS OF PEOPLE VISIT ACADIA EACH YEAR.

MILLIONS!

IF EVERYONE TOOK SOMETHING THAT BELONGED TO ACADIA,
THERE WOULD BE NOTHING LEFT.

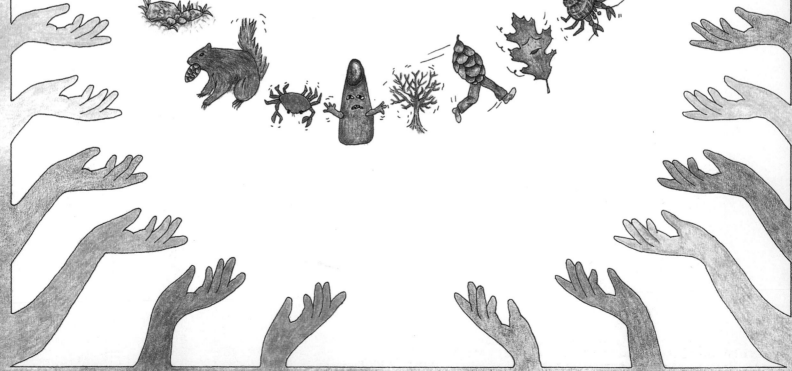

NATIONAL PARK MOTTO

ADD A LINE TO EACH LETTER TO SOLVE THE SECRET MESSAGE.
EXAMPLE: ∧⌐∧)·∧ = ACADIA

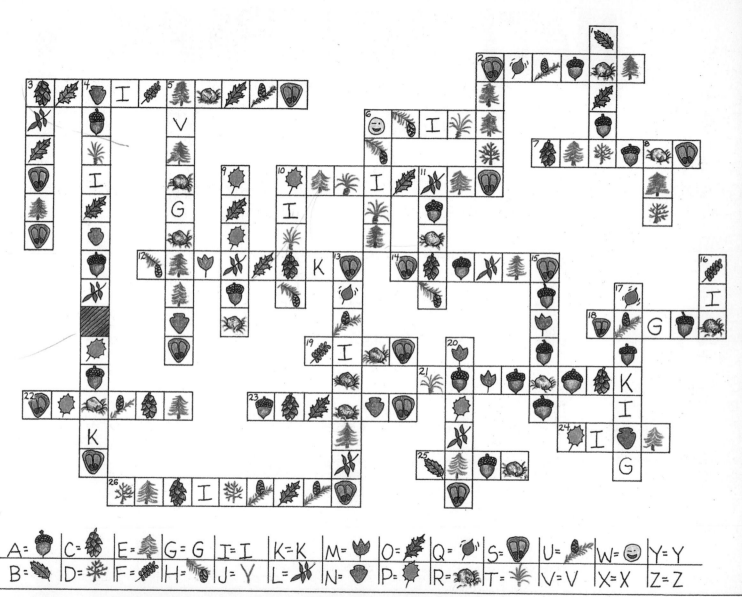

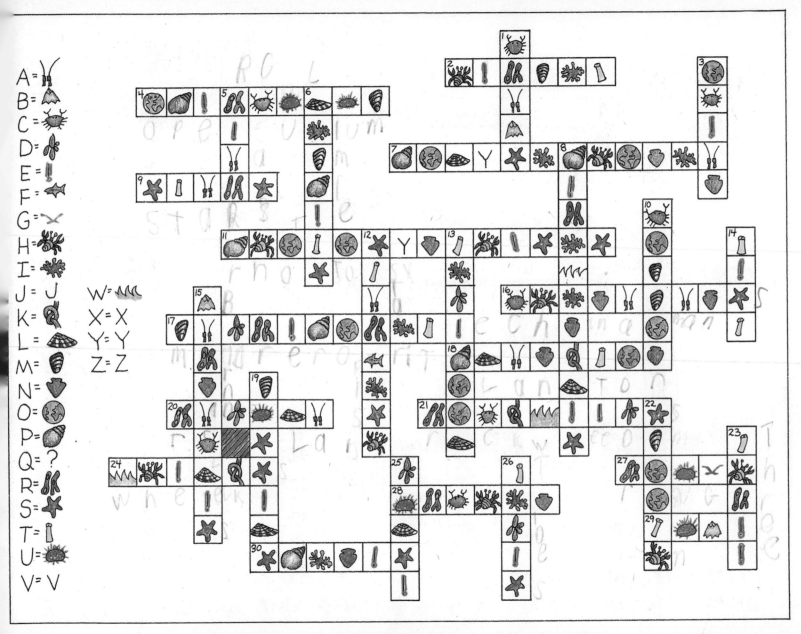

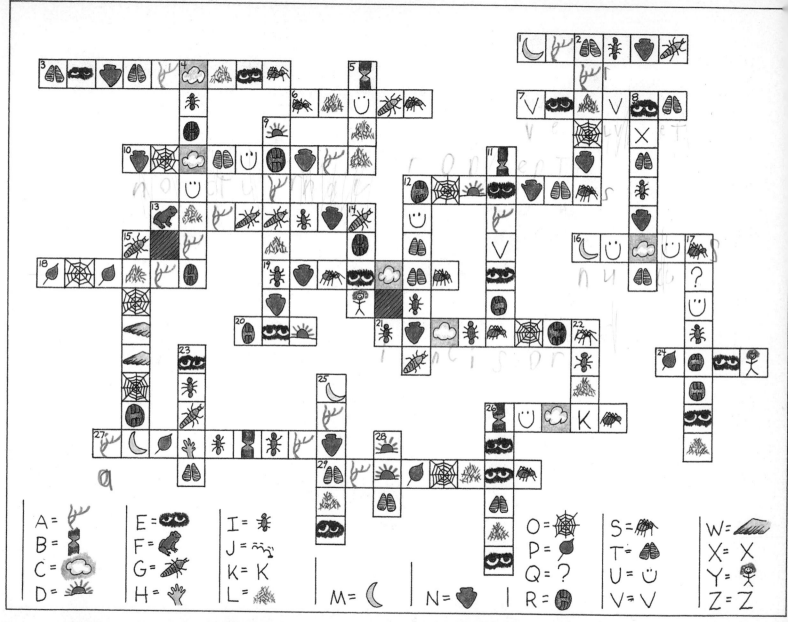

ANSWERS TO CRITTER CROSSWORD — PAGE 67.

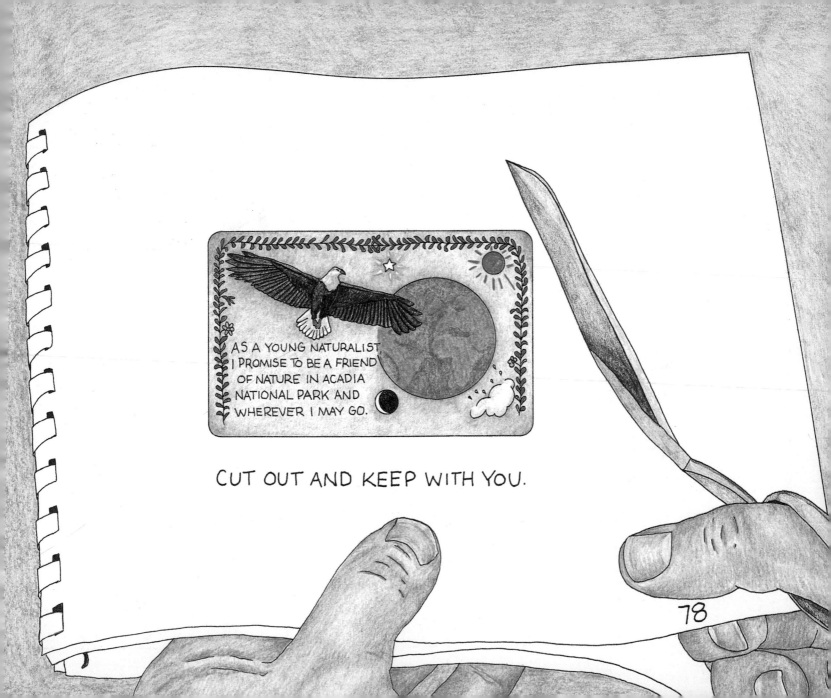

AS A YOUNG NATURALIST
I PROMISE TO BE A FRIEND
OF NATURE IN ACADIA
NATIONAL PARK AND
WHEREVER I MAY GO.

CUT OUT AND KEEP WITH YOU.

78

CARD IS NOT VALID UNLESS SIGNED.

TEAR OUT THE NEXT PAGE AND HANG IT UP AS YOUR VERY OWN POSTER.

MY NAME IS

_____

I AM A YOUNG NATURALIST

AND FRIEND OF ACADIA